COMPOSER SHOWCASE

HAL LEONARD
STUDENT PIANO LIBRARY

Impresiones de España

6 ORIGINAL PIANO SOLOS INSPIRED BY SPAIN

BY MONA REJINO

ISBN 978-1-5400-8748-5

HAL•LEONARD®

Visit Hal Leonard Online at
www.halleonard.com

Contact us:
Hal Leonard
7777 West Bluemound Road
Milwaukee, WI 53213
Email: info@halleonard.com

In Europe, contact:
Hal Leonard Europe Limited
42 Wigmore Street
Marylebone, London, W1U 2RN
Email: info@halleonardeurope.com

In Australia, contact:
Hal Leonard Australia Pty. Ltd.
4 Lentara Court
Cheltenham, Victoria, 3192 Australia
Email: info@halleonard.com.au

FROM THE COMPOSER

Impresiones de España (Impressions of Spain) was inspired by my recent travels to the central and southern parts of this intriguing country. In fact, the southern region of Andalusia inspired much of the music of Spanish composers. Each piece in this book represents a city or town that we explored and became acquainted with.

The people of Spain are gracious and joyful, celebrating and embracing life at every turn. They love to stroll and enjoy the beautiful evenings with their loved ones. Walking through the markets, the scent of spices fills the air. From the delicious and creative tapas found in restaurants to the tasty gelato on street corners, the cuisine of Spain is a delight. The many musicians performing on the streets and sharing their love of music with others moved me to do the same through these compositions.

The sights and sounds of Spain left an indelible impression, and I hope to return to Spain someday. In the meantime, my memories will be enhanced by the music it inspired.

La Alhambra de Granada
Granada celebrated its millennial (1000-year) anniversary as a kingdom in 2013. It was once the grandest city in Spain. The city rises from a plain onto three hills with the Sierra Nevada in the background. Its most revered sight is the Alhambra, a sprawling palace-fortress which represented the power of the Moorish kingdom for centuries. Within its massive walls are royal quarters, court chambers, baths, and elegant gardens.

Madrid (Ciudad Fantástico)
Madrid is located right in the center of Spain. Its bustling streets are filled with performing musicians and living-statue street performers, always entertaining the crowds of people who gather around them. One side of Madrid houses the lavish Royal Palace with its opulent 2800 rooms. Across town is the incomparable Prado Museum which houses paintings by Spanish artists Francisco de Goya, El Greco, and Diego Velázquez, among many others.

Malaga (Villa del Mar)
Malaga was the hometown of one of Spain's most revered artists, Pablo Picasso. It is a port city located on the Costa del Sol of the Mediterranean Sea, filled with lush vegetation and lots of sunshine. Many of the streets in Malaga are made of beautiful marble from the region, giving it a feel of elegance. Malaga's history spans about 2800 years, making it one of the oldest continuously inhabited cities in the world.

Ronda (Balada del Torero)
Ronda is one of many white hill towns found in Andalucía, full of character, charm, and history. It is the birthplace of modern bullfighting. Ronda's setting is breathtaking, as it literally hangs on a high cliff. The Guadalevín River runs through the city, dividing it in two and carving out the steep, 100-plus-meter-deep El Tajo canyon above which the city perches. Every building in this white hill town gleams in the bright sunshine which permeates the region.

Sevilla (Danza Flamenco)
Sevilla has been described as both flamboyant and soulful. *Flamenco* is a music and dance art form with roots in the Roma and Moorish cultures; its birthplace is Sevilla. Like jazz, flamenco thrives on improvisation. With a combination of percussive footwork and graceful hand gestures from the dancers, as well as technical proficiency from the guitarists and wails from the singers, you will never forget the flamenco experience.

Procesión de Toledo
Toledo, the spiritual center of Spain, sits atop a circular hill bounded on three sides by the Rio Tajo. Following its narrow winding streets leads to many hidden gems. Its magnificent cathedral sits in the center of town, towering over the city. During the height of its medieval history, Toledo was a haven of cultural diversity, with people of different faiths living together in harmony.

Mona Rejino

CONTENTS

La Alhambra de Granada

By Mona Rejino

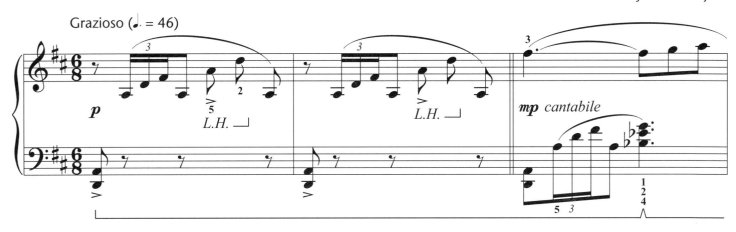

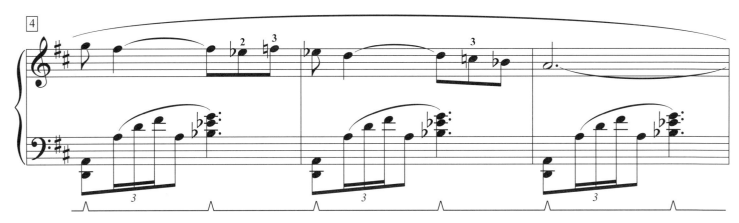

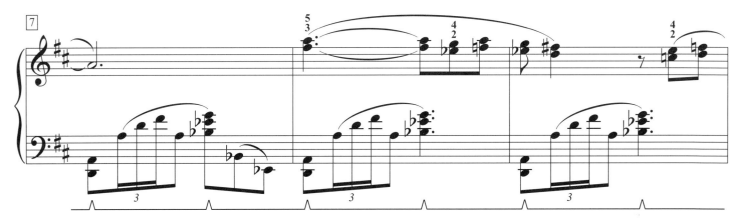

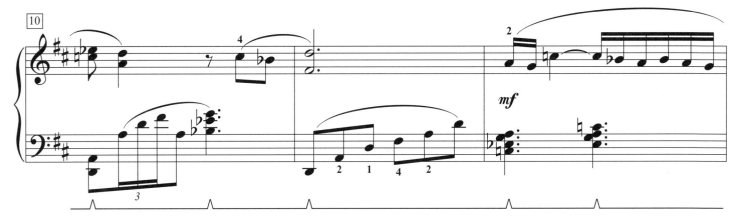

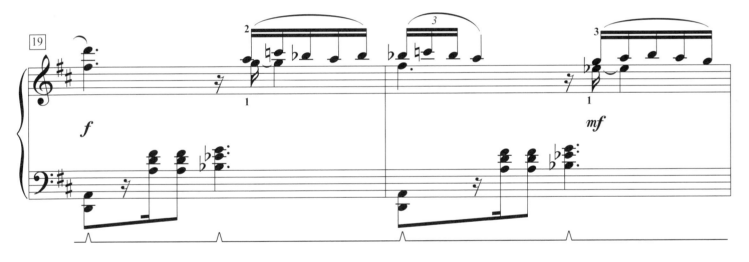

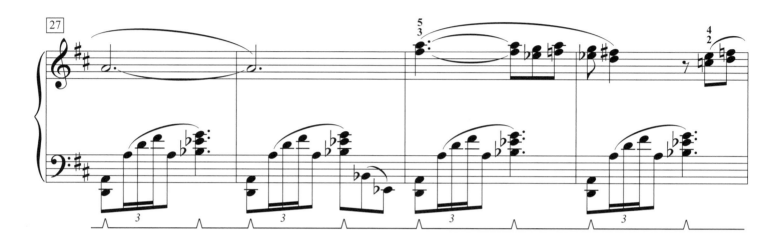

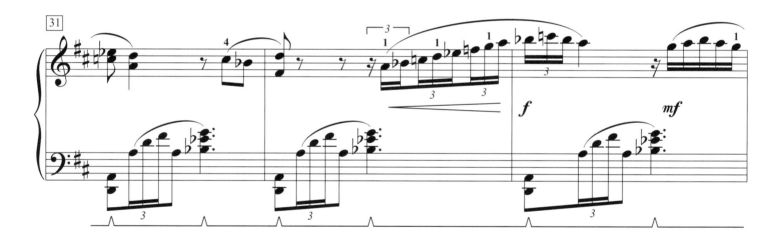

Malaga
(Villa del Mar)

By Mona Rejino

Andante (♩ = 104)

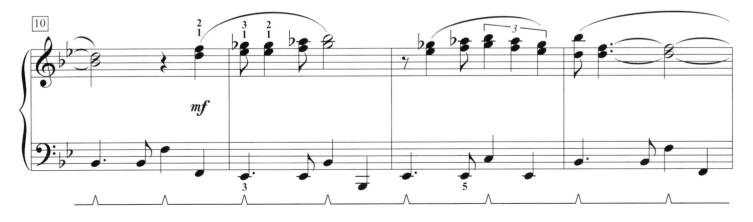

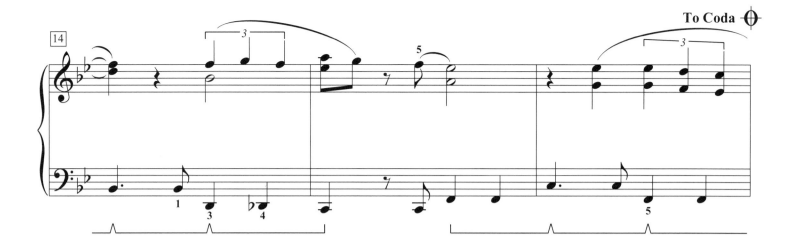

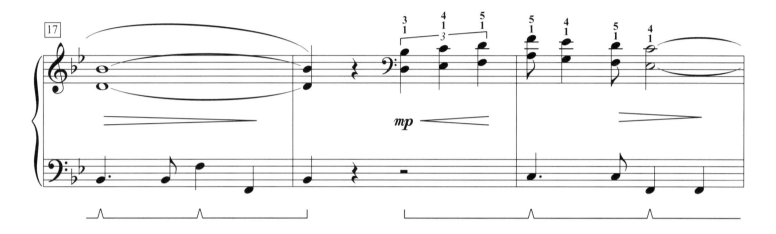

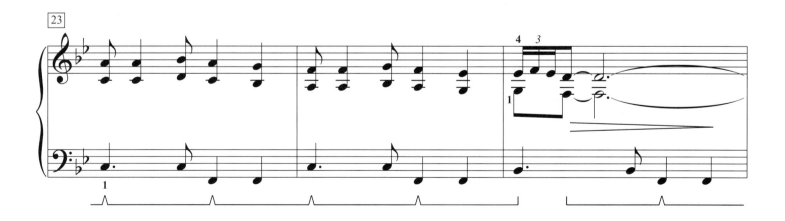

D.S. al Coda

CODA

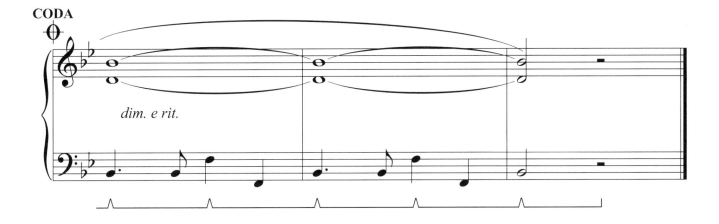

dim. e rit.

Madrid
(Ciudad Fantástico)

By Mona Rejino

Allegro e giocoso (♩. = 69)

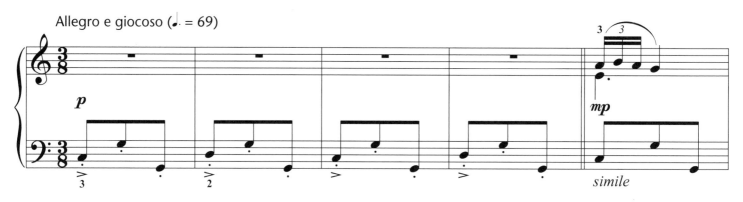

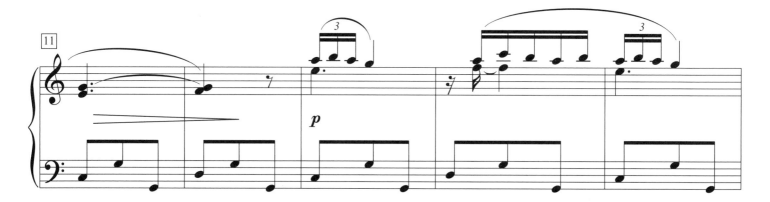

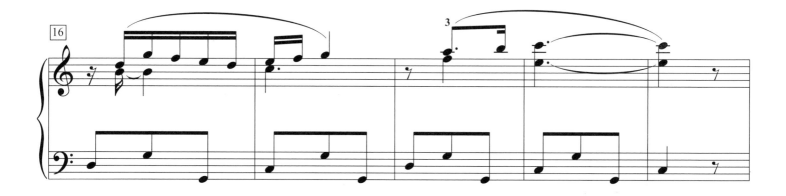

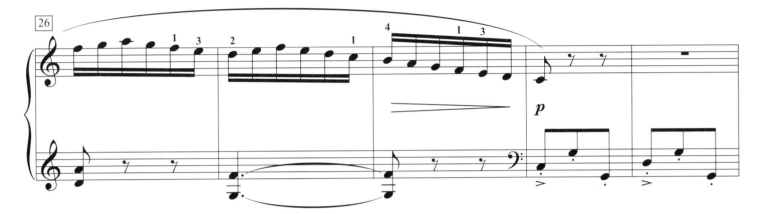

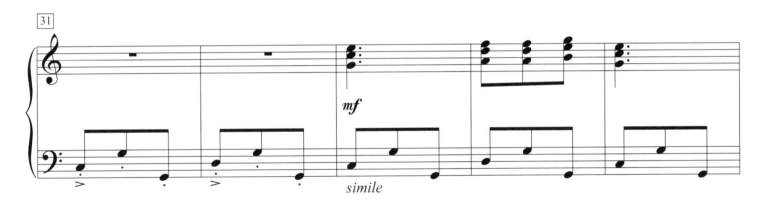

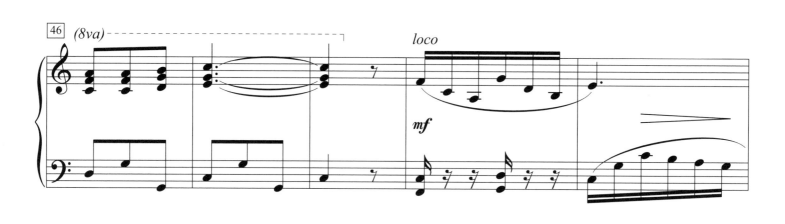

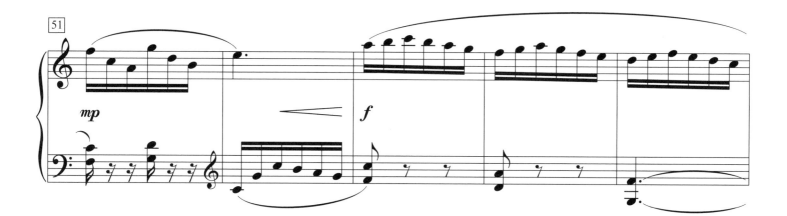

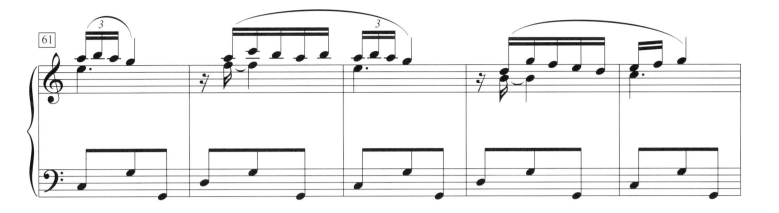

Procesión de Toledo

By Mona Rejino

Maestoso (♩ = 88)

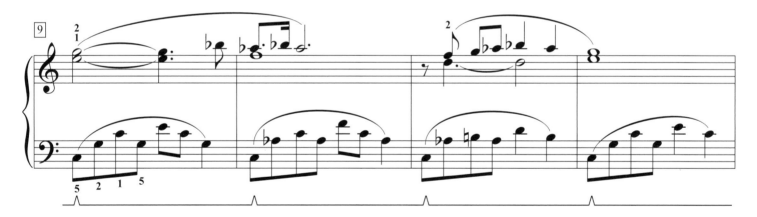

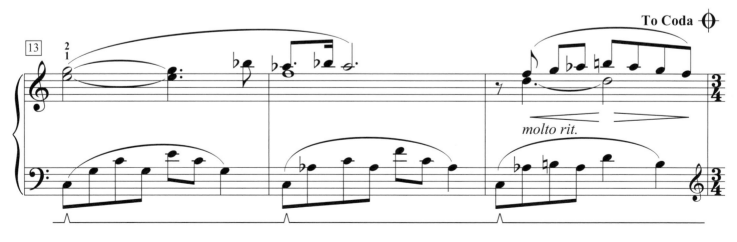

Dance-like (♩. = 72)

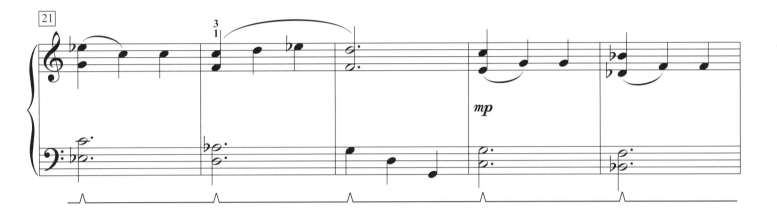

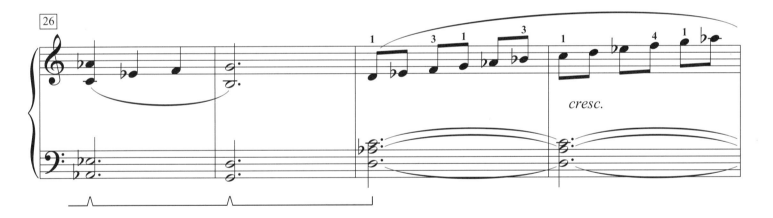

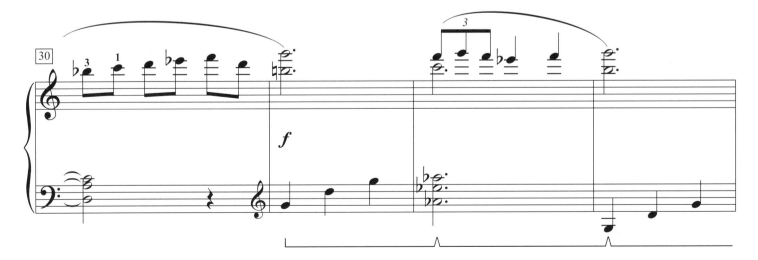

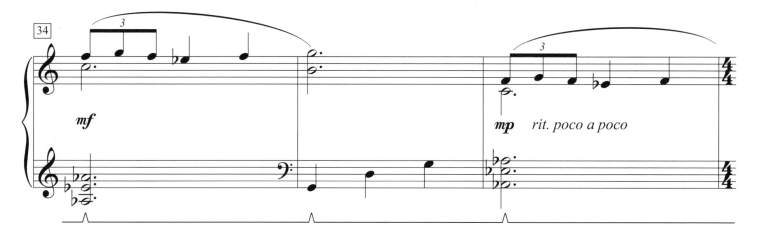

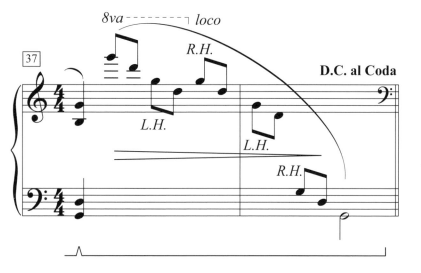

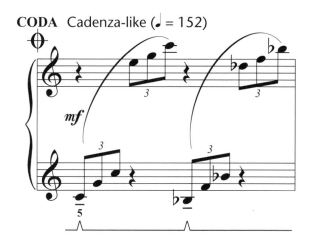

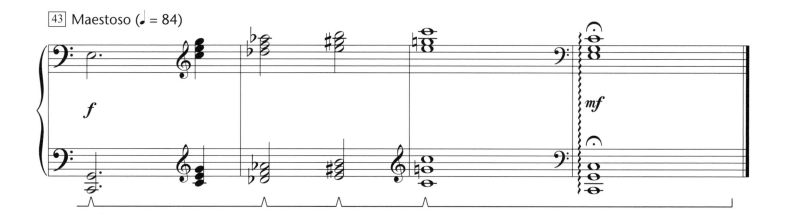

Ronda
(Balada del Torero)

By Mona Rejino

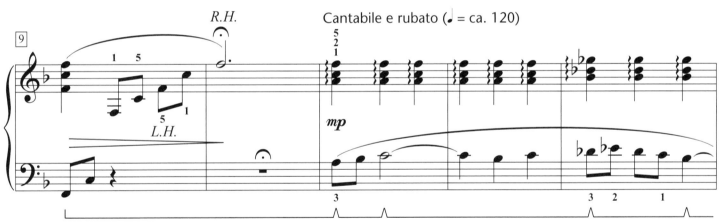

Tempo Primo

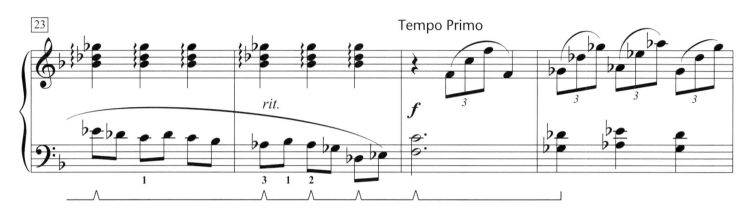

Cantabile e rubato (♩ = ca. 120)

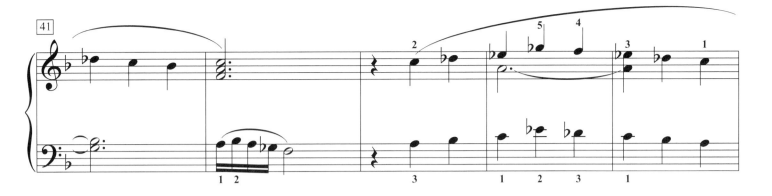

Tempo Primo

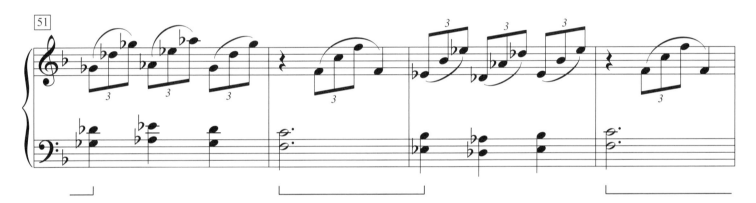

molto rit.

f

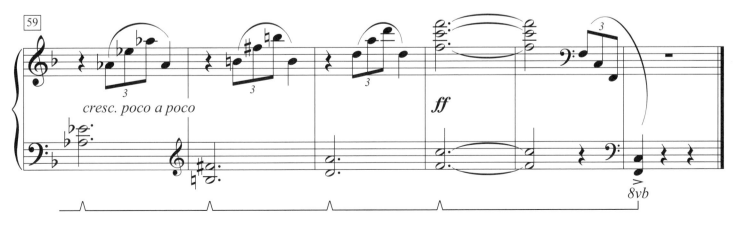

cresc. poco a poco

ff

8vb

19

Sevilla
(Danza Flamenco)

By Mona Rejino

Misterioso (♩ = 112)

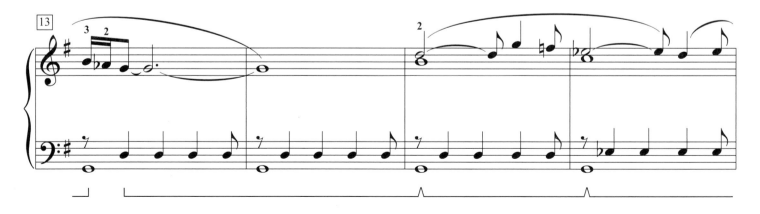

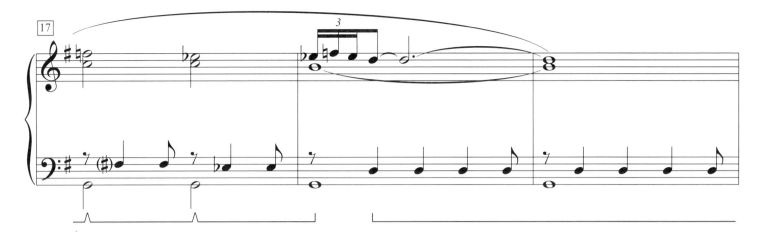

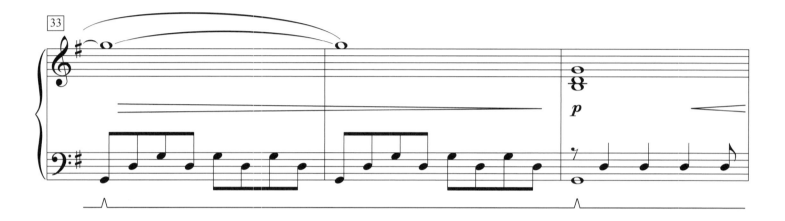

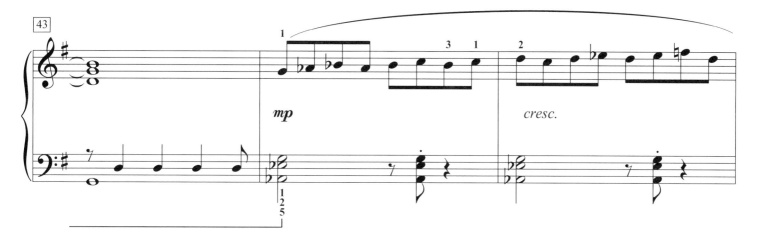